Tertullian

Against the Valentinians

Tertullian

Against the Valentinians

Tertullian
Against the Valentinians

Published by
Lighthouse Christian Publishing
SAN 257-4330
5531 Dufferin Drive
Savage, Minnesota, 55378
United States of America

www.lighthousechristianpublishing.com

Tertullian

Introductory Note.

The Second Class of Tertullian's works, according to the logical method I have endeavored to carry out, is that which includes his treatises against the heresies of his times. In these, the genius of our author is brilliantly illustrated, while, in melancholy fact, he is demonstrating the folly of his own final lapse and the wickedness of that schism and heresy into which he fell away from Truth. Were it not that history abounds in like examples of the frailty of the human intellect and of the insufficiency of "man that walketh to direct his steps," we should be forced to a theory of mental decay to account for inconsistencies so gross and for delusions so besotted. "Genius to madness is *indeed* allied," and who knows but something like that imbecility which closed the career of Swift may have been the fate of this splendid wit and versatile man of parts? Charity, admiration and love force this inquiry upon my own mind continually, as I explore his fascinating pages. And the order in which the student will find them in this series, will lead, I think, to similar reflections on the part of many readers. We observe a natural bent and turn of mind, even in his Catholic writings, which indicate his perils. These are more and more apparent in his recent works, as his enthusiasm heats itself into a frenzy which at last becomes a rage. He breaks down by degrees, as in orthodoxy so also in force and in character. It is almost like the collapse of Solomon or of Bacon. And though our own times have produced no example of stars of equal magnitude, to become falling-stars, we have seen illustrations the most humiliating, of those calm words of Bishop Kaye: "Human nature often presents the curious phenomenon of a union of the most opposite qualities in the same mind; of vigor, acuteness and discrimination on some subjects, with imbecility, dullness and bigotry on others." Milton, himself another example of his own threnode, breaks forth in this splendid utterance of lyrical confession:

> "God of our fathers what is man?
> Nor do I name of men the common rout,
> That, wandering loose about,
> Grow up and perish as the summer fly,
> Heads without name, no more remembered,
> But such as thou hast solemnly elected,
> With gifts and graces eminently adorned,
> To some great work, thy glory
> And people's safety, *which in part they effect.*"

And here, I must venture a remark on the ambiguity of the expressions concerning our author's Montanism. In the treatise against Marcion, written late in his career, Tertullian identifies himself with the Church and strenuously defends its faith and its apostolic order. In only rare instances does his weakness for the "new prophecy" crop out, and then, it is only as one identifies himself with a school within the church. Precisely so Fenelon maintained his milder Montanism, without a thought of deserting the Latin Church. Afterwards Fenelon drew back, but at last poor Tertullian fell away. So with the Jansenists. They credited the *miracles* and the *convulsions* (or ecstasies) of their school, and condemned those who rejected them, as Tertullian condemns the *Psychics*. The great expounder of the Nicene Faith (Bp. Bull) does indeed speak very decidedly of Tertullian as a *lapser*, even when he wrote his first book against Marcion. His semi-schismatic position must be allowed. But, was it a *formal* lapse at that time? The English non-jurors were long in communion with the Church, even while they denounced their brethren and the "Erastianizing" clergy, much as Tertullian does the *Psychics*. St. Augustine speaks of *Tertullianists* with great moderation, and notes the final downfall of our author as something distinct from Tertullianism. When we reflect, therefore, that only four of all his varied writings (now extant) are proofs of an accomplished lapse, ought we not carefully to maintain the distinction between the Montanistic Tertullian and Tertullian the Montanist? Bishop Bull, it seems to me would not object to this way of putting it, when we consider his own discrimination in the following weighty words. He says:

"A clear distinction must be made between those works which Tertullian, when already a Montanist, wrote specifically in defense of Montanism *against the church*, and those which he composed, as a Montanist indeed, yet *not in defense of Montanism against the church*, but rather, *in defense of the common doctrines of the church*—and of Montanus, in opposition to other heretics."

Now in arranging the works of this second class, *the Prescription* comes logically first, because, written in Orthodoxy, it forcibly upholds the Scriptural Rule of Faith, the Catholic touchstone of all professed verity. It is also a necessary Introduction to the great work against Marcion which I have placed next in order; giving it the precedence to which it is entitled in part on chronological ground, in part because of the general purity of its material with the exhibition it presents of the author's mental processes and of his very gradual decline from Truth.

Very fortunate were the Edinburgh Editors in securing for this work and some others, the valuable labors of Dr. Holmes, of whom I have elsewhere given some biographical

particulars. The merit and fullness of his annotations are so marked, that I have been spared a great deal of work, such as I was forced to bestow on the former volumes of this American Edition. But on the other hand these pages have given me much patient study and toil as an editor, because of the "shreds and patches" in which Tertullian comes to us, in the Edinburgh Series; and because of some typographical peculiarities, exceptional in that Series itself, and presenting complications, when transferred to a new form of mechanical arrangement.
For example, apart from some valuable material which belongs to the General Preface, and which I have transferred accordingly, the following dislocations confronted me to begin with: The *Marcion* is presented to us in Volume VII. apart from the other writings of Tertullian. At the close of Vol. XI. we reach the *Ad Nationes*, of which Dr. Holmes is the translator, another hand (Mr. Thelwall's) having been employed on former pages of that volume. It is not till we reach Volume XV. that Tertullian again appears, but this volume is wholly the work of Dr. Holmes. Finally, in Volume XVIII., we meet Tertullian again, (Mr. Thelwall the able translator), but, here is placed the "Introduction" to all the works of
Tertullian, which, of course, I have, transferred to its proper place. I make these explanations by no means censoriously, but to point out at once the nature of my own task, and the advantage that accrues to the reader, by the order in which the works of the great Tertullian appear in this edition, enabling him to compare different or parallel passages, all methodically arranged in consecutive pages, without a minute's search, or delay.

Now, as to typographical difficulties to which I have referred, Dr. Holmes marks all his multiplied and useful notes with *brackets*, which are almost always superfluous, and which in this American Edition are used to designate my own contributions, when printed with the text, or apart from Preface and Elucidations. These, therefore, I have removed necessarily and with no appreciable loss to the work, but great gain to the beauty of the page. But, again, Dr. Holmes' translations are all so heavily bracketed as to become an eyesore, and the disfigured pages have been often complained of as afflictive to the reader. Many words strictly implied by the original Latin, and which should therefore be unmarked, are yet put between brackets. Even minute words (*and*, or *to wit*, or *again*,) when, in the nature of the case the English idiom requires them, are thus marked. I have not retained these blemishes; but when an inconsiderable word or a repetition does add to the sense, or qualify it, I have italicized such words, throwing more important interpolations into parenthetical marks, which are less painful to the sight than brackets. I have found them quite as serviceable to denote the auxiliary word or phrase; and where the author himself uses a parenthesis, I have observed very few instances in which a sensible reader would confound it with the translator's efforts to eke out the sense. Sometimes, an awkward interpolation has been thrown into a footnote.

Occasionally the crabbed sentences of the great Carthaginian are so obscure that Dr. Holmes has been unable to make them lucid, although, with the original in hand, he probably felt a force in his own rendering which the mere English reader must fail to perceive. In a few such instances, noting the fact in the margin, I have tried to bring out the sense, by slight modifications of punctuation and arrangement. Occasionally too I have dropped a superfluous interpolation (such as *e.g.*, *to conclude*, or let me say again,) when I have found that it only served to clog and overcharge a sentence. Last of all, Dr. Holmes' *headings* have sometimes been condensed, to avoid phrases and sentences immediately recurring in the chapter. These purely mechanical parts require a terse form of statement, like those in the English Bible, and I have frequently reduced them on that model, dropping redundant adverbs and adjectives to bring out the catchwords.

Against the Valentinians.

In Which the Author Gives a Concise Account of, Together with Sundry Caustic Animadversions on, the Very Fantastic Theology of the Sect. This Treatise is Professedly Taken from the Writings of Justin, Miltiades, Irenæus, and Proculus.

Chapter I.—Introductory. Tertullian Compares the Heresy to the Old Eleusinian Mysteries. Both Systems Alike in Preferring Concealment of Error and Sin to Proclamation of Truth and Virtue.

The Valentinians, who are no doubt a very large body of heretics—comprising as they do so many apostates from the truth, who have a propensity for fables, and no discipline to deter them (therefrom) care for nothing so much as to obscure what they preach, if indeed they (can be said to) preach who obscure their doctrine. The officiousness with which they guard their doctrine is an officiousness which betrays their guilt. Their disgrace is proclaimed in the very earnestness with which they maintain their religious system. Now, in the case of those Eleusinian mysteries, which are the very heresy of Athenian superstition, it is their secrecy that is their disgrace. Accordingly, they previously beset all access to their body with tormenting conditions; and they require a long initiation before they enroll (their members), even instruction during five years for their perfect disciples, in order that they may mold their opinions by this suspension of full knowledge, and apparently raise the dignity of their mysteries in proportion to the craving for them which they have previously created. Then follows the duty of silence. Carefully is that guarded, which is so long in finding. All the divinity, however, lies in their secret recesses: there are revealed at last all the aspirations of the fully initiated, the entire mystery of the sealed tongue, the symbol of virility. But this allegorical representation, under the pretext of nature's reverend name, obscures a real sacrilege by help of an arbitrary symbol, and by empty images obviates the reproach of falsehood! In like manner, the heretics who are now the object of our remarks, the Valentinians, have formed Eleusinian dissipations of their own, consecrated by a profound silence, having nothing of the heavenly in them but their mystery. By the help of the sacred names and titles and arguments of true religion, they have fabricated the vainest and foulest figment for men's pliant liking, out of the affluent suggestions of Holy Scripture, since from its many springs many errors may well emanate. If you propose to them inquiries sincere and honest, they answer you with stern look and contracted brow, and say, "The subject is profound." If you try them with subtle questions, with the ambiguities of their double tongue, they affirm a community of faith (with yourself). If you intimate to them that you understand their opinions, they insist on knowing nothing themselves. If you come to a close engagement with them they destroy your own fond hope of a victory over them by a self-immolation. Not even to their own disciples do they commit a secret before they have made sure of them. They have the knack of persuading men before instructing them; although truth persuades by teaching, but does not teach by first persuading.

Chapter II.—These Heretics Brand the Christians as Simple Persons. The Charge Accepted, and Simplicity Eulogized Out of the Scriptures.

For this reason, we are branded by them as simple, and as being merely so, without being wise also; as if indeed wisdom were compelled to be wanting in simplicity, whereas the Lord unites them both: "Be ye therefore wise as serpents, and simple as doves." Now if we, on our parts, be accounted foolish because we are simple, does it then follow that they are not simple because they are wise? Most perverse, however, are they who are not simple, even as they are most foolish who are not wise. And yet, (if I must choose) I should prefer taking the latter condition for the lesser fault; since it is perhaps better to have a wisdom which falls short in quantity, than that which is bad in quality—better to be in error than to mislead. Besides, the face of the Lord is patiently waited for by those who "seek Him in simplicity of heart," as says the very Wisdom—not of Valentinus, but—of Solomon. Then, again, infants have borne by their blood a testimony to Christ. (Would you say) that it was children who shouted "Crucify Him"? They were neither children nor infants; in other words, they were not simple. The apostle, too, bids us to "become children again" towards God, "to be as children in malice" by our simplicity, yet as being also "wise in our practical faculties." At the same time, with respect to the order of development in Wisdom, I have admitted that it flows from simplicity. In brief, "the dove" has usually served to figure Christ; "the serpent," to tempt Him. The one even from the first has been the harbinger of divine peace; the other from the beginning has been the despoiler of the divine image. Accordingly, simplicity alone will be more easily able to know and to declare God, whereas wisdom alone will rather do Him violence, and betray Him.

Chapter III.—The Folly of This Heresy. It Dissects and Mutilates the Deity. Contrasted with the Simple Wisdom of True Religion. To Expose the Absurdities of the Valentinian System is to Destroy It.

Let, then, the serpent hide himself as much as he is able, and let him wrest all his wisdom in the labyrinths of his obscurities; let him dwell deep down in the ground; let him worm himself into secret holes; let him unroll his length through his sinuous joints; let him tortuously crawl, though not all at once, beast as he is that skulks the light. Of our dove, however, how simple is the very home!—always in high and open places, and facing the light! As the symbol of the Holy Spirit, it loves the (radiant) East, that figure of Christ. Nothing causes truth a blush, except only being hidden, because no man will be ashamed to give ear thereto. No man will be ashamed to recognize Him as God whom nature has already commended to him, whom he already perceives in all His works,—Him indeed who is simply, for this reason, imperfectly known; because man has not thought of Him as only one, because he has named Him in a plurality (of gods), and adored Him in other forms. Yet, to induce oneself to turn from this multitude of deities to another crowd, to remove from a familiar authority to an unknown one, to wrench oneself from what is manifest to what is hidden, is to offend faith on the very threshold. Now, even suppose that you are initiated into the entire fable, will it not occur to you that you have heard something very like it from your fond nurse when you were a baby, amongst the lullabies she sang to you about the towers of Lamia, and the horns of the sun? Let, however, any man approach the subject from a knowledge of the faith which he has otherwise learned, as soon as he finds so many names of Æons, so many marriages, so many offspring, so many exits, so many issues, felicities and infelicities of a dispersed and mutilated Deity, will that man hesitate at once to pronounce that these are "the fables and endless genealogies" which the inspired apostle by anticipation condemned, whilst these seeds of heresy were even then shooting forth? Deservedly, therefore, must they be regarded as wanting in simplicity, and as merely prudent, who produce such fables not without difficulty, and defend them only indirectly, who at the same time do not thoroughly instruct those whom they teach. This, of course, shows their astuteness, if their lessons are disgraceful; their unkindness, if they are honorable. As for us, however, who are the simple folk, we know all about it. In short, this is the very first weapon with which we are armed for our encounter; it unmasks and brings to view the whole of their depraved system. And in this we have the first augury of our victory; because even merely to point out that which is concealed with so great an outlay of artifice, is to destroy it.

Chapter IV.—The Heresy Traceable to Valentinus, an Able But Restless Man. Many Schismatical Leaders of the School Mentioned. Only One of Them Shows Respect to the Man Whose Name Designates the Entire School.

We know, I say, most fully their actual origin, and we are quite aware why we call them Valentinians, although they affect to disavow their name. They have departed, it is true, from their founder, yet is their origin by no means destroyed; and even if it chance to be changed, the very change bears testimony to the fact. Valentinus had expected to become a bishop, because he was an able man both in genius and eloquence. Being indignant, however, that another obtained the dignity by reason of a claim which confessorship had given him, he broke with the church of the true faith. Just like those (restless) spirits which, when roused by ambition, are usually inflamed with the desire of revenge, he applied himself with all his might to exterminate the truth; and finding the clue of a certain old opinion, he marked out a path for himself with the subtlety of a serpent. Ptolemæus afterwards entered on the same path, by distinguishing the names and the numbers of the Ænons into personal substances, which, however, he kept apart from God. Valentinus had included these in the very essence of the Deity, as senses and affections of motion. Sundry bypaths were then struck off therefrom, by Heraclean and Secundus and the magician Marcus. Theotimus worked hard about "the images of the law." Valentinus, however, was as yet nowhere, and still the Valentinians derive their name from Valentinus. Axionicus at Antioch is the only man who at the present time does honor to the memory of Valentinus, by keeping his rules to the full. But this heresy is permitted to fashion itself into as many various shapes as a courtesan, who usually changes and adjusts her dress every day. And why not? When they review that spiritual seed of theirs in every man after this fashion, whenever they have hit upon any novelty, they forthwith call their presumption a revelation, their own perverse ingenuity a spiritual gift; but (they deny all) unity, admitting only diversity. And thus we clearly see that, setting aside their customary dissimulation, most of them are in a divided state, being ready to say (and that sincerely) of certain points of their belief, "This is not so;" and, "I take this in a different sense;" and, "I do not admit that." By this variety, indeed, innovation is stamped on the very face of their rules; besides which, it wears all the colorable features of ignorant conceits.

Chapter V.—Many Eminent Christian Writers Have Carefully and Fully Refuted the Heresy. These the Author Makes His Own Guides.

My own path, however, lies along the original tenets of their chief teachers, not with the self-appointed leaders of their promiscuous followers. Nor shall we hear it said of us from any quarter, that we have of our own mind fashioned our own materials, since these have been already produced, both in respect of the opinions and their refutations, in carefully written volumes, by so many eminently holy and excellent men, not only those who have lived before us, but those also who were contemporary with the heresiarchs themselves: for instance Justin, philosopher and martyr; Miltiades, the sophist of the churches; Irenæus, that very exact inquirer into all doctrines; our own Proculus, the model of chaste old age and Christian eloquence. All these it would be my desire closely to follow in every work of faith, even as in this particular one. Now if there are no heresies at all but what those who refute them are supposed to have fabricated, then the apostle who predicted them must have been guilty of falsehood. If, however, there are heresies, they can be no other than those which are the subject of discussion. No writer can be supposed to have so much time on his hands as to fabricate materials which are already in his possession.

Chapter VI.—Although Writing in Latin He Proposes to Retain the Greek Names of the Valentinian Emanations of Deity. Not to Discuss the Heresy But Only to Expose It. This with the Raillery Which Its Absurdity Merits.

In order then, that no one may be blinded by so many outlandish names, collected together, and adjusted at pleasure, and of doubtful import, I mean in this little work, wherein we merely undertake to propound this (heretical) mystery, to explain in what manner we are to use them. Now the rendering of some of these names from the Greek so as to produce an equally obvious sense of the word, is by no means an easy process: in the case of some others, the genders are not suitable; while others, again, are more familiarly known in their Greek form. For the most part, therefore, we shall use the Greek names; their meanings will be seen on the margins of the pages. Nor will the Greek be unaccompanied with the Latin equivalents; only these will be marked in lines above, for the purpose of explaining the personal names, rendered necessary by the ambiguities of such of them as admit some different meaning. But although I must postpone all discussion, and be content at present with the mere exposition (of the heresy), still, wherever any scandalous feature shall seem to require a castigation, it must be attacked by all means, if only with a passing thrust. Let the reader regard it as the skirmish before the battle. It will be my drift to show how to wound rather than to inflict deep gashes. If in any instance mirth be excited, this will be quite as much as the subject deserves. There are many things which deserve refutation in such a way as to have no gravity expended on them. Vain and silly topics are met with especial fitness by laughter. Even the truth may indulge in ridicule, because it is jubilant; it may play with its enemies, because it is fearless. Only we must take care that its laughter be not unseemly, and so itself be laughed at; but wherever its mirth is decent, there it is a duty to indulge it. And so at last I enter on my task.

Chapter VII.—The First Eight Emanations, or Æons, Called the Ogdoad, are the Fountain of All the Others. Their Names and Descent Recorded.

Beginning with Ennius, the Roman poet, he simply spoke of "the spacious saloons of heaven,"—either on account of their elevated site, or because in Homer he had read about Jupiter banqueting therein. As for our heretics, however, it is marvelous what stories upon stories and what heights upon heights, they have hung up, raised and spread out as a dwelling for each several god of theirs. Even our Creator has had arranged for Him the saloons of Ennius in the fashion of private rooms, with chamber piled upon chamber, and assigned to each god by just as many staircases as there were heresies. The universe, in fact, has been turned into "rooms to let." Such stories of the heavens you would imagine to be detached tenements in some happy isle of the blessed, I know not where. There the god even of the Valentinians has his dwelling in the attics. They call him indeed, as to his essence, Αἰῶν τέλειος (Perfect Æon), but in respect of his personality, Προαρχή (Before the Beginning), Ἡ Ἀρχή (The Beginning), and sometimes Bythos (Depth), a name which is most unfit for one who dwells in the heights above! They describe him as unbegotten, immense, infinite, invisible, and eternal; as if, when they described him to be such as we know that he ought to be, they straightway prove him to be a being who may be said to have had such an existence even before all things else. I indeed insist upon it that he is such a being; and there is nothing which I detect in beings of this sort more obvious, than that they who are said to have been before all things—things, too, not their own—are found to be behind all things. Let it, however, be granted that this Bythos of theirs existed in the infinite ages of the past in the greatest and profoundest repose, in the extreme rest of a placid and, if I may use the expression, stupid divinity, such as Epicurus has enjoined upon us. And yet, although they would have him be alone, they assign to him a second person in himself and with himself, Ennoea (Thought), which they also call both Charis (Grace) and Sige (Silence). Other things, as it happened, conduced in this most agreeable repose to remind him of the need of by and by producing out of himself the beginning of all things. This he deposits in lieu of seed in the genital region, as it were, of the womb of his Sige. Instantaneous conception is the result: Sige becomes pregnant, and is delivered, of course in silence; and her offspring is Nus (Mind), very like his father and his equal in every respect. In short, he alone is capable of comprehending the measureless and incomprehensible greatness of his father. Accordingly, he is even called the Father himself, and the Beginning of all things, and, with great propriety, Monogenes (The Only-begotten). And yet not with absolute propriety, since he is not born alone. For along with him a female also proceeded, whose name was Veritas (Truth). But how much more suitably might Monogenes be called Protogenes (First begotten), since he was begotten first! Thus Bythos and Sige, Nus and Veritas, are alleged to be the first fourfold team of the Valentinian set (of gods) the parent stock and origin of them all. For immediately when Nus received the function of a procreation of his own, he too produces out of himself Sermo (the Word) and Vita (the Life). If this latter existed not previously, of course she existed not in Bythos. And a pretty absurdity would it be, if Life existed not in God! However, this offspring also produces fruit, having for its mission the initiation of the universe and the formation of the entire Pleroma: it procreates Homo (Man) and Ecclesia (the Church). Thus you have an Ogdoad, a double Tetra, out of the conjunctions of males and females—the cells (so to speak) of the primordial Æons, the fraternal nuptials of the Valentinian gods, the simple originals of heretical sanctity and majesty, a rabble—shall I say of criminals or of deities?—at any rate, the fountain of all ulterior fecundity.

Chapter VIII.—The Names and Descent of Other Æons; First Half a Score, Then Two More, and Ultimately a Dozen Besides. These Thirty Constitute the Pleroma. But Why Be So Capricious as to Stop at Thirty?

For, behold, when the second Tetrad—Sermo and Vita, Homo and Ecclesia—had borne fruit to the Father's glory, having an intense desire of themselves to present to the Father something similar of their own, they bring other issue into being—conjugal of course, as the others were—by the union of the twofold nature. On the one hand, Sermo and Vita pour out at a birth a half-score of Æons; on the other hand, Homo and Ecclesia produce a couple more, so furnishing an equipoise to their parents, since this pair with the other ten make up just as many as they did themselves procreate. I now give the names of the half-score whom I have mentioned: Bythios (Profound) and Mixis (Mixture), Ageratos (Never old) and Henosis (Union), Autophyes (Essential nature) and Hedone (Pleasure), Acinetos (Immoveable) and Syncrasis (Commixture,) Monogenes (Only-begotten) and Macaria (Happiness). On the other hand, these will make up the number twelve (to which I have also referred): Paracletus (Comforter) and Pistis (Faith), Patricas (Paternal) and Elpis (Hope), Metricos (Maternal) and Agape (Love), Ainos (Praise)and Synesis (Intelligence), Ecclesiasticus (Son of Ecclesia) and Macariotes (Blessedness), Theletus (Perfect) and Sophia (Wisdom). I cannot help here quoting from a like example what may serve to show the import of these names. In the schools of Carthage there was once a certain Latin rhetorician, an excessively cool fellow, whose name was Phosphorus. He was personating a man of valor, and wound up with saying, "I come to you, excellent citizens, from battle, with victory for myself, with happiness for you, full of honor, covered with glory, the favorite of fortune, the greatest of men, decked with triumph." And forthwith his scholars begin to shout for the school of Phosphorus, φεῦ (ah!). Are you a believer in Fortunata, and

Hedone, and Acinetus, and Theletus? Then shout out your φεῦfor the school of Ptolemy. This must be that mystery of the Pleroma, the fullness of the thirty-fold divinity. Let us see what special attributes belong to these numbers—four, and eight, and twelve. Meanwhile with the number thirty all fecundity ceases. The generating force and power and desire of the Æons is spent. As if there were not still left some strong rennet for curdling numbers. As if no other names were to be got out of the page's hall! For why are there not sets of fifty and of a hundred procreated? Why, too, are there no comrades and boon companions named for them?

Chapter IX.—Other Capricious Features in the System. The Æons Unequal in Attributes. The Superiority of Nus; The Vagaries of Sophia Restrained by Horos. Grand Titles Borne by This Last Power.

But, further, there is an "acceptance of persons," inasmuch as Nus alone among them all enjoys the knowledge of the immeasurable Father, joyous and exulting, while they of course pine in sorrow. To be sure, Nus, so far as in him lay, both wished and tried to impart to the others also all that he had learnt about the greatness and incomprehensibility of the Father; but his mother, Sige, interposed—she who (you must know) imposes silence even on her own beloved heretics; although they affirm that this is done at the will of the Father, who will have all to be inflamed with a longing after himself. Thus, while they are tormenting themselves with these internal desires, while they are burning with the secret longing to know the Father, the crime is almost accomplished. For of the twelve Æons which Homo and Ecclesia had produced, the youngest by birth (never mind the solecism, since Sophia (Wisdom) is her name), unable to restrain herself, breaks away without the society of her husband Theletus, in quest of the Father and contracts that kind of sin which had indeed arisen amongst the others who were conversant with Nus but had flowed on to this

Æon, that is, to Sophia; as is usual with maladies which, after arising in one part of the body, spread abroad their infection to some other limb. The fact is, under a presence of love to the Father, she was overcome with a desire to rival Nus, who alone rejoiced in the knowledge of the Father. But when Sophia, straining after impossible aims, was disappointed of her hope, she is both overcome with difficulty, and racked with affection. Thus she was all but swallowed up by reason of the charm and toil (of her research), and dissolved into the remnant of his substance; nor would there have been any other alternative for her than perdition, if she had not by good luck fallen in with Horus (Limit). He too had considerable power. He is the foundation of the great universe, and, externally, the guardian thereof. To him they give the additional names of Crux (Cross), and Lytrotes (Redeemer,) and Carpistes (Emancipator). When Sophia was thus rescued from danger, and tardily persuaded, she relinquished further research after the Father, found repose, and laid aside all her excitement, or Enthymesis (Desire,) along with the passion which had come over her.

Chapter X.—Another Account of the Strange Aberrations of Sophia, and the Restraining Services of Horus. Sophia Was Not Herself, After All, Ejected from the Pleroma, But Only Her Enthymesis.

But some dreamers have given another account of the aberration and recovery of Sophia. After her vain endeavors, and the disappointment of her hope, she was, I suppose, disfigured with paleness and emaciation, and that neglect of her beauty which was natural to one who was deploring the denial of the Father,—an affliction which was no less painful than his loss. Then, in the midst of all this sorrow, she by herself alone, without any conjugal help, conceived and bare a female offspring. Does this excite your surprise? Well, even the hen has the power of being able to bring forth by her own energy. They say, too, that among vultures there are only females, which become parents alone. At any rate, she was another without aid from a male, and she began at last to be afraid that her end was even at hand. She was all in doubt about the treatment of her case, and took pains at self-concealment. Remedies could nowhere be found. For where, then, should we have tragedies and comedies, from which to borrow the process of exposing what has been born without connubial modesty? While the thing is in this evil plight, she raises her eyes, and turns them to the Father. Having, however, striven in vain, as her strength was failing her, she falls to praying. Her entire kindred also supplicate in her behalf, and especially Nus. Why not? What was the cause of so vast an evil? Yet not a single casualty befell Sophia without its effect. All her sorrows operate. Inasmuch as all that conflict of hers contributes to the origin of Matter. Herignorance, her fear, her distress, become substances. Hereupon the Father by and by, being moved, produces in his own image, with a view to these circumstances the Horos whom we have mentioned above; (and this he does) by means of Monogenes Nus, a male-female (Æon), because there is this variation of statement about the Father's sex. They also go on to tell us that Horos is likewise called Metagogius, that is, "a conductor about," as well as Horothetes (Setter of Limits). By his assistance they declare that Sophia was checked in her illicit courses, and purified from all evils, and henceforth strengthened (in virtue), and restored to the conjugal state: (they add) that she indeed remained within the bounds of the Pleroma, but that her Enthymesis, with the accruing Passion, was banished by Horos, and crucified and cast out from the Pleroma,—even as they say, Malum foras! (Evil, avaunt!) Still, that was a spiritual essence, as being the natural impulse of an Æon, although without form or shape, inasmuch as it had apprehended nothing, and therefore was pronounced to be an infirm and feminine fruit.

Chapter XI.—The Profane Account Given of the Origin of Christ and the Holy Ghost Sternly Rebuked. An Absurdity Respecting the Attainment of the Knowledge of God Ably Exposed.

Accordingly, after the banishment of the Enthymesis, and the return of her mother Sophia to her husband, the (illustrious) Monogenes, the Nus, released indeed from all care and concern of the Father, in order that he might consolidate all things, and defend and at last fix the Pleroma, and so prevent any concussion of the kind again, once more emits a new couple (blasphemously named). I should suppose the coupling of two males to be a very shameful thing, or else the one must be a female, and so the male is discredited by the female. One divinity is assigned in the case of all these, to procure a complete adjustment among the Æons. Even from this fellowship in a common duty two schools actually arise, two chairs, and, to some extent, the inauguration of a division in the doctrine of Valentinus. It was the function of Christ to instruct the Æons in the nature of their conjugal relations (you see what the whole thing was, of course!), and how to form some guess about the unbegotten, and to give them the capacity of generating within themselves the knowledge of the Father; it being impossible to catch the idea of him, or comprehend him, or, in short, even to enjoy any perception of him, either by the eye or the ear, except through Monogenes (the Only-begotten). Well, I will even grant them what they allege about knowing the Father, so that they do not refuse us (the attainment of) the same. I would rather point out what is perverse in their doctrine, how they were taught that the incomprehensible part of the Father was the cause of their own perpetuity, whilst that which might be comprehended of him was the reason of their generation and formation. Now by these several positions the tenet, I suppose, is insinuated, that it is expedient for God not to be apprehended, on the very ground that the incomprehensibility of His character is the cause of perpetuity;

whereas what in Him is comprehensible is productive, not of perpetuity, but rather of conditions which lack perpetuity—namely, nativity and formation. The Son, indeed, they made capable of comprehending the Father. The manner in which He is comprehended, the recently produced Christ fully taught them. To the Holy Spirit, however, belonged the special gifts, whereby they, having been all set on a complete par in respect of their earnestness to learn, should be enabled to offer up their thanksgiving, and be introduced to a true tranquility.

Chapter XII.—The Strange Jumble of the Pleroma. The Frantic Delight of the Members Thereof. Their Joint Contribution of Parts Set Forth with Humorous Irony.

Thus they are all on the self-same footing in respect of form and knowledge, all of them having become what each of them severally is; none being a different being, because they are all what the others are. They are all turned into Nuses, into Homos, into Theletuses; and so in the case of the females, into Siges, into Zoes, into Ecclesias, into Fortunatas, so that Ovid would have blotted out his own Metamorphoses if he had only known our larger one in the present day. Straightway they were reformed and thoroughly established, and being composed to rest from the truth, they celebrate the Father in a chorus of praise in the exuberance of their joy. The Father himself also reveled in the glad feeling; of course, because his children and grandchildren sang so well. And why should he not revel in absolute delight? Was not the Pleroma freed (from all danger)? What ship's captain fails to rejoice even with indecent frolic? Every day we observe the uproarious ebullitions of sailors' joys. Therefore, as sailors always exult over the reckoning they pay in common, so do these Æons enjoy a similar pleasure, one as they now all are in form, and, as I may add, in feeling too. With the concurrence of even their new brethren and masters, they contribute into one common stock the best and most beautiful thing with which they are severally adorned. Vainly, as I suppose. For if they were all one by reason by the above-mentioned thorough equalization, there was no room for the process of a common reckoning, which for the most part consists of a pleasing variety. They all contributed the one good thing, which they all were. There would be, in all probability, a formal procedure in the mode or in the form of the very equalization in question. Accordingly, out of the donation which they contributed to the honor and glory of the Father, they jointly fashion the most beautiful constellation of the Pleroma, and its perfect fruit, Jesus. Him they also surname Soter (Savior) and Christ, and Sermo (Word) after his ancestors; and lastly Omnia (All Things), as formed from a universally culled nosegay, like the jay of Æsop, the Pandora of Hesiod, the bowl of Accius, the honeycake of Nestor, the miscellany of Ptolemy. How much nearer the mark, if these idle title mongers had called him Pancarpian, after certain Athenian customs. By way of adding external honor also to their wonderful puppet, they produce for him a bodyguard of angels of like nature. If this be their mutual condition, it may be all right; if, however, they are consubstantial with Soter (for I have discovered how doubtfully the case is stated), where will be his eminence when surrounded by attendants who are co-equal with himself?

Chapter XIII.—First Part of the Subject, Touching the Constitution of the Pleroma, Briefly Recapitulated. Transition to the Other Part, Which is Like a Play Outside the Curtain.

In this series, then, is contained the first emanation of Æons, who are alike born, and are married, and produce offspring: there are the most dangerous fortunes of Sophia in her ardent longing for the Father, the most seasonable help of Horos, the expiation of her Enthymesis and accruing Passion, the instruction of Christ and the Holy Spirit, their tutelar reform of the Æons, the piebald ornamentation of Soter, the consubstantial retinue of the angels. All that remains, according to you, is the fall of the curtain and the clapping of hands. What remains in my opinion, however, is, that you should hear and take heed. At all events, these things are said to have been played out within the company of the Pleroma, the first scene of the tragedy. The rest of the play, however, is beyond the curtain—I mean outside of the Pleroma. And yet if it be such within the bosom of the Father, within the embrace of the guardian Horos, what must it be outside, in free space, where God did not exist?

Chapter XIV.—The Adventures of Achamoth Outside the Pleroma. The Mission of Christ in Pursuit of Her. Her Longing for Christ. Horos' Hostility to Her. Her Continued Suffering.

For Enthymesis, or rather Achamoth—because by this inexplicable name alone must she be henceforth designated—when in company with the vicious Passion, her inseparable companion, she was expelled to places devoid of that light which is the substance of the Pleroma, even to the void and empty region of Epicurus, she becomes wretched also because of the place of her banishment. She is indeed without either form or feature, even an untimely and abortive production. Whilst she is in this plight, Christ descends from the heights, conducted by Horos, in order to impart form to the abortion, out of his own energies, the form of substance only, but not of knowledge also. Still she is left with some property. She has restored to her the odor of immortality, in order that she might, under its influence, be overcome with the desire of better things than belonged to her present plight. Having accomplished His merciful mission, not without the assistance of the Holy Spirit, Christ returns to the Pleroma. It is usual out of an abundance of things for names to be also forthcoming. Enthymesis came from action; whence Achamoth came is still a question; Sophia emanates from the Father, the Holy Spirit from an angel. She entertains a regret for Christ immediately after she had discovered her desertion by him. Therefore she hurried forth herself, in quest of the light of Him Whom she did not at all discover, as He operated in an invisible manner; for how else would she make search for His light, which was as unknown to her as He was Himself? Try, however, she did, and perhaps would have found Him, had not the self-same Horos, who had met her mother so opportunely, fallen in with the daughter quite as unseasonably, so as to exclaim at her Iao! just as we hear the cry "Porro Quirites" ("Out of the way, Romans!"), or else Fidem Cæsaris!" ("By the faith of Cæsar!"), whence (as they will have it) the name Iaocomes to be found is the Scriptures. Being thus hindered from proceeding further, and being unable to sur mount the Cross, that is to say, Horos, because she had not yet practiced herself in the part of Catullus' Laureolus, and given over, as it were, to that passion of hers in a manifold and complicated mesh, she began to be afflicted with every impulse thereof, with sorrow,—because she had not accomplished her enterprise, with fear,—lest she should lose her life, even as she had lost the light, with consternation, and then with ignorance. But not as her mother (did she suffer this), for she was an Æon. Hers, however, was a worse suffering, considering her condition; for another tide of emotion still overwhelmed her, even of conversion to the Christ, by Whom she had been restored to life, and had been directed to this very conversion.

Chapter XV.—Strange Account of the Origin of Matter, from the Various Affections of Achamoth. The Waters from Her Tears; Light from Her Smile.

Well, now, the Pythagoreans may learn, the Stoics may know, Plato himself (may discover), whence Matter, which they will have to be unborn, derived both its origin and substance for all this pile of the world—(a mystery) which not even the renowned Mercurius Trismegistus, master (as he was) of all physical philosophy, thought out. You have just heard of

“Conversion,” one element in the “Passion” (we have so often mentioned). Out of this the whole life of the world, and even that of the Demiurge himself, our God, is said to have had its being. Again, you have heard of “sorrow” and “fear.” From these all other created things took their beginning. For from her tears flowed the entire mass of waters. From this circumstance one may form an idea of the calamity which she encountered, so vast were the kinds of the tears wherewith she overflowed. She had salt teardrops, she had bitter, and sweet, and warm, and cold, and bituminous, and ferruginous, and sulphurous, and even poisonous, so that the Nonacris exuded therefrom which killed Alexander; and the river of the Lyncestæ flowed from the same source, which produces drunkenness; and the Salmacis was derived from the same source, which renders men effeminate. The rains of heaven Achamoth whimpered forth, and we on our part are anxiously employed in saving up in our cisterns the very wails and tears of another. In like manner, from the “consternation” and “alarm” (of which we have also heard), bodily elements were derived. And yet amidst so many circumstances of solitude, in this vast prospect of destitution, she occasionally smiled at the recollection of the sight of Christ, and from this smile of joy light flashed forth. How great was this beneficence of Providence, which induced her to smile, and all that we might not linger for ever in the dark! Nor need you feel astonished how from her joy so splendid an element could have beamed upon the world, when from her sadness even so necessary a provision flowed forth for man. O illuminating smile! O irrigating tear! And yet it might now have acted as some alleviation amidst the horror of her situation; for she might have shaken off all the obscurity thereof as often as she had a mind to smile, even not to be obliged to turn suppliant to those who had deserted her.

Chapter XVI.—Achamoth Purified from All Impurities of Her Passion by the Paraclete, Acting Through Soter, Who Out of the Above-Mentioned Impurities Arranges Matter, Separating Its Evil from the Better Qualities.

She, too, resorts to prayers, after the manner of her mother. But Christ, Who now felt a dislike to quit the Pleroma, appoints the Paraclete as his deputy. To her, therefore, he dispatches Soter, (who must be the same as Jesus, to whom the Father imparted the supreme power over the whole body of the Æons, by subjecting them all to him, so that "by him," as the apostle says, "all things were created"), with a retinue and cortege of contemporary angels, and (as one may suppose) with the dozen fasces. Hereupon Achamoth, being quite struck with the pomp of his approach, immediately covered herself with a veil, moved at first with a dutiful feeling of veneration and modesty; but afterwards she surveys him calmly, and his prolific equipage. With such energies as she had derived from the contemplation, she meets him with the salutation, Κύριε, χαῖρε("Hail, Lord")! Upon this, I suppose, he receives her, confirms and conforms her in knowledge, as well as cleanses her from all the outrages of Passion, without, however, utterly severing them, with an indiscriminateness like that which had happened in the casualties which befell her mother. For such vices as had become inveterate and confirmed by practice he throws together; and when he had consolidated them in one mass, he fixes them in a separate body, so as to compose the corporeal condition of Matter, extracting out of her inherent, incorporeal passion such an aptitude of nature as might qualify it to attain to a reciprocity of bodily substances, which should emulate one another, so that a twofold condition of the substances might be arranged; one full of evil through its faults, the other susceptible of passion from conversion. This will prove to be Matter, which has set us in battle array against Hermogenes, and all others who presume to teach that God made all things out of Matter, not out of nothing.

Chapter XVII.—Achamoth in Love with the Angels. A Protest Against the Lascivious Features of Valentinianism. Achamoth Becomes the Mother of Three Natures.

Then Achamoth, delivered at length from all her evils, wonderful to tell goes on and bears fruit with greater results. For warmed with the joy of so great an escape from her unhappy condition, and at the same time heated with the actual contemplation of the angelic luminaries (one is ashamed) to use such language, (but there is no other way of expressing one's meaning), she during the emotion somehow became personally inflamed with desire towards them, and at once grew pregnant with a spiritual conception, at the very image of which the violence of her joyous transport, and the delight of her prurient excitement had imbibed and impressed upon her. She at length gave birth to an offspring, and then there arose a leash of natures, from a triad of causes,—one material, arising from her passion; another animal, arising from her conversion; the third spiritual, which had its origin in her imagination.

Chapter XVIII.—Blasphemous Opinion Concerning the Origin of the Demiurge, Supposed to Be the Creator of the Universe.

Having become a better proficient in practical conduct by the authority which, we may well suppose, accrued to her from her three children, she determined to impart form to each of the natures. The spiritual one however, she was unable to touch, inasmuch as she was herself spiritual. For a participation in the same nature has, to a very great extent, disqualified like and consubstantial beings from having superior power over one another. Therefore, she applies herself solely to the animal nature, adducing the instructions of Soter (for her guidance). And first of all (she does) what cannot be described and read, and heard of, without an intense horror at the blasphemy thereof: she produces this God of ours, the God of all except of the heretics, the Father and Creator and King of all things, which are inferior to him. For from him do they proceed. If, however, they proceed from him, and not rather from Achamoth, or if only secretly from her, without his perceiving her, he was impelled to all that he did, even like a puppet which is moved from the outside. In fact, it was owing to this very ambiguity about the personal agency in the works which were done, that they coined for him the mixed name of (Motherly Father), whilst his other appellations were distinctly assigned according to the conditions and positions of his works: so that they call him Fatherin relation to the animal substances to which they give the place of honor on his right hand; whereas, in respect of the material substances which they banish to his left hand, they name him Demiurgus; whilst his title Kingdesignates his authority over both classes, nay over the universe.

Chapter XIX.—Palpable Absurdities and Contradictions in the System Respecting Achamoth and the Demiurge.

And yet there is not any agreement between the propriety of the names and that of the works, from which all the names are suggested; since all of them ought to have borne the name of her by whom the things were done, unless after all it turn out that they were not made by her. For, although they say that Achamoth devised these forms in honor of the Æons, they yet transfer this work to Soter as its author, when they say that he operated through her, so far as to give her the very image of the invisible and unknown Father—that is, the image which was unknown and invisible to the Demiurge; whilst he formed this same Demiurge in imitation of Nus the son of Propator; and whilst the archangels, who were the work of the Demiurge, resembled the other Æons. Now, when I hear of such images of the three, I ask, do you not wish me to laugh at these pictures of their most extravagant painter? At the female Achamoth, a picture of the Father? At the Demiurge, ignorant of his mother, much more so of his father? At the picture of Nus, ignorant of his father too, and the ministering angels, facsimiles of their lords? This is painting a mule from an ass, and sketching Ptolemy from Valentinus.

Chapter XX—The Demiurge Works Away at Creation, as the Drudge of His Mother Achamoth, in Ignorance All the While of the Nature of His Occupation.

The Demiurge therefore, placed as he was without the limits of the Pleroma in the ignominious solitude of his eternal exile, founded a new empire—this world (of ours)—by clearing away the confusion and distinguishing the difference between the two substances which severally constituted it, the animal and the material. Out of incorporeal (elements) he constructs bodies, heavy, light, erect and stooping, celestial and terrene. He then completes the sevenfold stages of heaven itself, with his own throne above all. Whence he had the additional name of Sabbatum from the hebdomadal nature of his abode; his mother Achamoth, too, had the title Ogdoada, after the precedent of the primeval Ogdoad. These heavens, however, they consider to be intelligent, and sometimes they make angels of them, as indeed they do of the Demiurge himself; as also (they call) Paradise the fourth archangel, because they fix it above the third heaven, of the power of which Adam partook, when he sojourned there amidst its fleecy clouds and shrubs. Ptolemy remembered perfectly well the prattle of his boyhood, that apples grew in the sea, and fishes on the tree; after the same fashion, he assumed that nut-trees flourished in the skies. The Demiurge does his work in ignorance, and therefore perhaps he is unaware that trees ought to be planted only on the ground. His mother, of course, knew all about it: how is it, then, that she did not suggest the fact, since she was actually executing her own operation? But whilst building up so vast an edifice for her son by means of those works, which proclaim him at once to be father, god and, king before the conceits of the Valentinians, why she refused to let them be known to even him, is a question which I shall ask afterwards.

Chapter XXI.—The Vanity as Well as Ignorance of the Demiurge. Absurd Results from So Imperfect a Condition.

Meanwhile you must believe that Sophia has the surnames of earth and of Mother—"Mother-Earth," of course—and (what may excite your laughter still more heartily) even Holy Spirit. In this way they have conferred all honor on that female, I suppose even a beard, not to say other things. Besides, the Demiurge had so little mastery over things, on the score, you must know, of his inability to approach spiritual essences, (constituted as he was) of animal elements, that, imagining himself to be the only being, he uttered this soliloquy: "I am God, and beside me there is none else." But for all that, he at least was aware that he had not himself existed before. He understood, therefore, that he had been created, and that there must be a creator of a creature of some sort or other. How happens it, then, that he seemed to himself to be the only being, notwithstanding his uncertainty, and although he had, at any rate, some suspicion of the existence of some creator?

Chapter XXII.—Origin of the Devil, in the Criminal Excess of the Sorrow of Achamoth. The Devil, Called Also Munditenens, Actually Wiser Than the Demiurge, Although His Work.

The odium felt amongst them against the devil is the more excusable, even because the peculiarly sordid character of his origin justifies it. For he is supposed by them to have had his origin in that criminal excess of her sorrow, from which they also derive the birth of the angels, and demons, and all the wicked spirits. Yet they affirm that the devil is the work of the Demiurge, and they call him Munditenens (Ruler of the World), and maintain that, as he is of a spiritual nature, he has a better knowledge of the things above than the Demiurge, an animal being. He deserves from them the pre-eminence which all heresies provide him with.

Chapter XXIII.—The Relative Positions of the Pleroma. The Region of Achamoth, and the Creation of the Demiurge. The Addition of Fire to the Various Elements and Bodies of Nature.

Their most eminent powers, moreover, they confine within the following limits, as in a citadel. In the most elevated of all summits presides the tricenary Pleroma, Horos marking off its boundary line. Beneath it, Achamoth occupies the intermediate space for her abode, treading down her son. For under her comes the Demiurge in his own Hebdomad, or rather the Devil, sojourning this world in common with ourselves, formed, as has been said above, of the same elements and the same body, out of the most profitable calamities of Sophia; inasmuch as, (if it had not been for these,) our spirit would have had no space for inhaling and ejecting air—that delicate vest of all corporeal creatures, that revealer of all colors, that instrument of the seasons—if the sadness of Sophia had not filtered it, just as her fear did the animal existence, and her conversion the Demiurge himself. Into all these elements and bodies fire was fanned. Now, since they have not as yet explained to us the original sensation of this in Sophia, I will on my own responsibility conjecture that its spark was struck out of the delicate emotions of her (feverish grief). For you may be quite sure that, amidst all her vexations, she must have had a good deal of fever.

Chapter XXIV.—The Formation of Man by the Demiurge. Human Flesh Not Made of the Ground, But of a Nondescript Philosophic Substance.

Such being their conceits respecting God, or, if you like, the gods, of what sort are their figments concerning man? For, after he had made the world, the Demiurge turns his hands to man, and chooses for him as his substance not any portion of "the dry land," as they say, of which alone we have any knowledge (although it was, at that time, not yet dried by the waters becoming separated from the earthy residuum, and only afterwards became dry), but of the invisible substance of that matter, which philosophy indeed dreams of, from its fluid and fusible composition, the origin of which I am unable to imagine, because it exists nowhere. Now, since fluidity and fusibility are qualities of liquid matter, and since everything liquid flowed from Sophia's tears, we must, as a necessary conclusion, believe that muddy earth is constituted of Sophia's eye-rheums and viscid discharges, which are just as much the dregs of tears as mud is the sediment of waters. Thus does the Demiurge mold man as a potter does his clay, and animates him with his own breath. Made after his image and likeness, he will therefore be both material and animal. A fourfold being! For in respect of his "image," he must be deemed clayey, that is to say, material, although the Demiurge is not composed of matter; but as to his "likeness," he is animal, for such, too, is the Demiurge. You have two (of his constituent elements). Moreover, a coating of flesh was, as they allege, afterwards placed over the clayey substratum, and it is this tunic of skin which is susceptible of sensation.

Chapter XXV.—An Extravagant Way of Accounting for the Communication of the Spiritual Nature to Man. It Was Furtively Managed by Achamoth, Through the Unconscious Agency of Her Son.

In Achamoth, moreover, there was inherent a certain property of a spiritual germ, of her mother Sophia's substance; and Achamoth herself had carefully severed off (the same quality), and implanted it in her son the Demiurge, although he was actually unconscious of it. It is for you to imagine the industry of this clandestine arrangement. For to this end had she deposited and concealed (this germ), that, whenever the Demiurge came to impart life to Adam by his inbreathing, he might at the same time draw off from the vital principle the spiritual seed, and, as by a pipe, inject it into the clayey nature; in order that, being then fecundated in the material body as in a womb, and having fully grown there, it might be found fit for one day receiving the perfect Word. When, therefore, the Demiurge commits to Adam the transmission of his own vital principle, the spiritual man lay hid, although inserted by his breath, and at the same time introduced into the body, because the Demiurge knew no more about his mother's seed than about herself. To this seed they give the name of Ecclesia (the Church), the mirror of the church above, and the perfection of man; tracing this perfection from Achamoth, just as they do the animal nature from the Demiurge, the clayey material of the body (they derive) from the primordial substance, the flesh from Matter. So that you have a new Geryon here, only a fourfold (rather than a threefold) monster.

Chapter XXVI.—The Three Several Natures—The Material, the Animal, and the Spiritual, and Their Several Destinations. The Strange Valentinian Opinion About the Structure of Soter's Nature.

In like manner they assign to each of them a separate end. To the material, that is to say the carnal (nature), which they also call "the left-handed," they assign undoubted destruction; to the animal (nature), which they also call "the right-handed," a doubtful issue, inasmuch as it oscillates between the material and the spiritual, and is sure to fall at last on the side to which it has mainly gravitated. As regards the spiritual, however, (they say) that it enters into the formation of the animal, in order that it may be educated in company with it and be disciplined by repeated intercourse with it. For the animal (nature) was in want of training even by the senses: for this purpose, accordingly, was the whole structure of the world provided; for this purpose also did Soter (the Savior) present Himself in the world—even for the salvation of the animal (nature). By yet another arrangement they will have it that He, in some prodigious way, clothed Himself with the primary portions of those substances, the whole of which He was going to restore to salvation; in such wise that He assumed the spiritual nature from Achamoth, whilst He derived the animal (being), Christ, afterwards from the Demiurge; His corporal substance, however, which was constructed of an animal nature (only with wonderful and indescribable skill), He wore for a dispensational purpose, in order that He might, in spite of His own unwillingness, be capable of meeting persons, and of being seen and touched by them, and even of dying. But there was nothing material assumed by Him, inasmuch as that was incapable of salvation. As if He could possibly have been more required by any others than by those who were in want of salvation! And all this, in order that by severing the condition of our flesh from Christ they may also deprive it of the hope of salvation!

Chapter XXVII.—The Christ of the Demiurge, Sent into the World by the Virgin. Not of Her. He Found in Her, Not a Mother, But Only a Passage or Channel. Jesus Descended Upon Christ, at His Baptism, Like a Dove; But, Being Incapable of Suffering, He Left Christ to Die on the Cross Alone.

I now adduce (what they say) concerning Christ, upon whom some of them engraft Jesus with so much license, that they foist into Him a spiritual seed together with an animal inflatus. Indeed, I will not undertake to describe these incongruous crammings, which they have contrived in relation both to their men and their gods. Even the Demiurge has a Christ of His own—His natural Son. An animal, in short, produced by Himself, proclaimed by the prophets—His position being one which must be decided by prepositions; in other words, He was produced by means of a virgin, rather than of a virgin! On the ground that, having descended into the virgin rather in the manner of a passage through her than of a birth by her, He came into existence through her, not of her—not experiencing a mother in her, but nothing more than a way. Upon this same Christ, therefore (so they say), Jesus descended in the sacrament of baptism, in the likeness of a dove. Moreover, there was even in Christ accruing from Achamoth the condiment of a spiritual seed, in order of course to prevent the corruption of all the other stuffing. For after the precedent of the principal Tetrad, they guard him with four substances—the spiritual one of Achamoth, the animal one of the Demiurge, the corporeal one, which cannot be described, and that of Soter, or, in other phrase, the columbine. As for Soter (Jesus), he remained in Christ to the last, impassible, incapable of injury, incapable of apprehension. By and by, when it came to a question of capture, he departed from him during the examination before Pilate. In like manner, his mother's seed did not admit of being injured, being equally exempt from all manner of outrage, and being undiscovered even by the Demiurge himself. The animal and carnal Christ, however, does suffer after the fashion of the superior Christ, who, for the purpose of producing Achamoth, had been stretched upon the cross, that is, Horos, in a substantial though not a cognizable form. In this manner do they reduce all things to mere images—Christians themselves being indeed nothing but imaginary beings!

Chapter XXVIII.—The Demiurge Cured of His Ignorance by the Savior's Advent, from Whom He Hears of the Great Future in Store for Himself.

Meanwhile the Demiurge, being still ignorant of everything, although he will actually have to make some announcement himself by the prophets, but is quite incapable of even this part of his duty (because they divide authority over the prophets between Achamoth, the Seed, and the Demiurge), no sooner heard of the advent of Soter (Savior) than he runs to him with haste and joy, with all his might, like the centurion in the Gospel. And being enlightened by him on all points, he learns from him also of his own prospect how that he is to succeed to his mother's place. Being thenceforth free from all care, he carries on the administration of this world, mainly under the plea of protecting the church, for as long a time as may be necessary and proper.

Chapter XXIX.—The Three Natures Again Adverted to. They are All Exemplified Amongst Men. For Instance, by Cain, and Abel, and Seth.

I will now collect from different sources, by way of conclusion, what they affirm concerning the dispensation of the whole human race. Having at first stated their views as to man's threefold nature—which was, however, united in one in the case of Adam—they then proceed after him to divide it (into three) with their especial characteristics, finding opportunity for such distinction in the posterity of Adam himself, in which occurs a threefold division as to moral differences. Cain and Abel, and Seth, who were in a certain sense the sources of the human race, become the fountain-heads of just as many qualities of nature and essential character. The material nature, which had become reprobate for salvation, they assign to Cain; the animal nature, which was poised between divergent hopes, they find in Abel; the spiritual, preordained for certain salvation, they store up in Seth. In this way also they make a twofold distinction among souls, as to their property of good and evil—according to the material condition derived from Cain, or the animal from Abel. Men's spiritual state they derive over and above the other conditions, from Seth adventitiously, not in the way of nature, but of grace, in such wise that Achamoth infuses it among superior beings like rain into good souls, that is, those who are enrolled in the animal class. Whereas the material class—in other words, those which are bad souls—they say, never receive the blessings of salvation; for that nature they have pronounced to be incapable of any change or reform in its natural condition. This grain, then, of spiritual seed is modest and very small when cast from her hand, but under her instruction increases and advances into full conviction, as we have already said; and the souls, on this very account, so much excelled all others, that the Demiurge, even then in his ignorance, held them in great esteem. For it was from their list that he had been accustomed to select men for kings and for priests; and these even now, if they have once attained to a full and complete knowledge of these foolish conceits of theirs, since they are already naturalized in the fraternal bond of the spiritual state, will obtain a sure salvation, nay, one which is on all accounts their due.

Chapter XXX.—The Lax and Dangerous Views of This Sect Respecting Good Works. That These are Unnecessary to the Spiritual Man.

For this reason, it is that they neither regard works as necessary for themselves, nor do they observe any of the calls of duty, eluding even the necessity of martyrdom on any presence which may suit their pleasure. For this rule, (they say), is enjoined upon the animal seed, in order that the salvation, which we do not possess by any privilege of our state, we may work out by right of our conduct. Upon us, who are of an imperfect nature, is imprinted the mark of this (animal) seed, because we are reckoned as sprung from the loves of Theletus, and consequently as an abortion, just as their mother was. But woe to us indeed, should we in any point transgress the yoke of discipline, should we grow dull in the works of holiness and justice, should we desire to make our confession anywhere else, I know not where, and not before the powers of this world at the tribunals of the chief magistrates! As for them, however, they may prove their nobility by the dissoluteness of their life and their diligence in sin, since Achamoth fawns on them as her own; for she, too, found sin no unprofitable pursuit. Now it is held amongst them, that, for the purpose of honoring the celestial marriages, it is necessary to contemplate and celebrate the mystery always by cleaving to a companion, that, is to a woman; otherwise (they account any man) degenerate, and a bastard to the truth, who spends his life in the world without loving a woman or uniting himself to her. Then what is to become of the eunuchs whom we see amongst them?

Chapter XXXI.—At the Last Day Great Changes Take Place Amongst the Æons as Well as Among Men. How Achamoth and the Demiurge are Affected Then. Irony on the Subject.

It remains that we say something about the end of the world, and the dispensing of reward. As soon as Achamoth has completed the full harvest of her seed, and has then proceeded to gather it into her garner, or, after it has been taken to the mill and ground to flour, has hidden it in the kneading-trough with yeast until the whole be leavened, then shall the end speedily come. Then, to begin with, Achamoth herself removes from the middle region, from the second stage to the highest, since she is restored to the Pleroma: she is immediately received by that paragon of perfection Soter, as her spouse of course, and they two afterwards consummate new nuptials. This must be the spouse of the Scripture, the Pleroma of espousals (for you might suppose that the Julian laws were interposing, since there are these migrations from place to place). In like manner, the Demiurge, too, will then change the scene of his abode from the celestial Hebdomad to the higher regions, to his mother's now vacant saloon—by this time knowing her, without however seeing her. (A happy coincidence!) For if he had caught a glance of her, he would have preferred never to have known her.

Chapter XXXII.—Indignant Irony Exposing the Valentinian Fable About the Judicial Treatment of Mankind at the Last Judgment. The Immorality of the Doctrine.

As for the human race, its end will be to the following effect:—To all which bear the earthy and material mark there accrues an entire destruction, because "all flesh is grass," and amongst these is the soul of mortal man, except when it has found salvation by faith. The souls of just men, that is to say, our souls, will be conveyed to the Demiurge in the abodes of the middle region. We are duly thankful; we shall be content to be classed with our god, in whom lies our own origin. Into the palace of the Pleroma nothing of the animal nature is admitted—nothing but the spiritual swarm of Valentinus. There, then, the first process is the despoiling of men themselves, that is, men within the Pleroma. Now this despoiling consists of the putting off of the souls in which they appear to be clothed, which they will give back to their Demiurge as they had obtained them from him. They will then become wholly intellectual spirits impalpable, invisible—and in this state will be readmitted invisibly to the Pleroma—stealthily, if the case admits of the idea. What then? They will be dispersed amongst the angels, the attendants on Soter. As sons, do you suppose? Not at all. As servants, then? No, not even so. Well, as phantoms? Would that it were nothing more! Then in what capacity, if you are ashamed to tell us? In the capacity of brides. Then will they end their Sabine rapes with the sanction of wedlock. This will be the guerdon of the spiritual, this the recompense of their faith! Such fables have their use. Although but a Marcus or a Gaius, full-grown in this flesh of ours, with a beard and such like proofs (of virility,) it may be a stern husband, a father, a grandfather, a great-grandfather (never mind what, in fact, if only a male), you may perhaps in the bridal chamber of the Pleroma—I have already said so tacitly—even become the parent by an angel of some Æon of high numerical rank. For the right celebration of these nuptials, instead of the torch and veil, I suppose that secret fire is then to burst forth, which, after devastating the whole existence of things, will itself also be reduced to nothing at last, after everything has been reduced to ashes; and so their fable too will be ended. But I, too, am no doubt a rash man, in having exposed so great a mystery in so derisive a way: I ought to be afraid that Achamoth, who did not choose to make herself known even to her own son, would turn mad, that Theletus would be enraged, that Fortune would be irritated. But I am yet a liege-man of the Demiurge. I have to return after death to the place where there is no more giving in marriage, where I have to be clothed upon rather than to be despoiled,—where, even if I am despoiled of my sex, I am classed with angels—not a male angel, nor a female one. There will be no one to do aught against me, nor will they then find any male energy in me.

Chapter XXXIII.—These Remaining Chapters an Appendix to the Main Work. In This Chapter Tertullian Notices a Difference Among Sundry Followers of Ptolemy, a Disciple of Valentinus.

I shall now at last produce, by way of finale, after so long a story, those points which, not to interrupt the course of it, and by the interruption distract the reader's attention, I have preferred reserving to this place. They have been variously advanced by those who have improved on the doctrines of Ptolemy. For there have been in his school "disciples above their master," who have attributed to their Bythus two wives—Cogitatio (Thought) and Voluntas (Will). For Cogitatio alone was not sufficient wherewith to produce any offspring, although from the two wives procreation was most easy to him. The former bore him Monogenes (Only-Begotten) and Veritas (Truth). Veritas was a female after the likeness of Cogitatio; Monogenes a male bearing a resemblance to Voluntas. For it is the strength of Voluntas which procures the masculine nature, inasmuch as she affords efficiency to Cogitatio.

Chapter XXXIV.—Other Varying Opinions Among the Valentinians Respecting the Deity, Characteristic Raillery.

Others of purer mind, mindful of the honor of the Deity, have, for the purpose of freeing him from the discredit of even single wedlock, preferred assigning no sex whatever to Bythus; and therefore very likely they talk of "this deity" in the neuter gender rather than "this god." Others again, on the other hand, speak of him as both masculine and feminine, so that the worthy chronicler Fenestella must not suppose that a hermaphrodite was only to be found among the good people of Luna.

Chapter XXXV.—Yet More Discrepancies. Just Now the Sex of Bythus Was an Object of Dispute; Now His Rank Comes in Question. Absurd Substitutes for Bythus Criticized by Tertullian.

There are some who do not claim the first place for Bythus, but only a lower one. They put their Ogdoad in the foremost rank; itself, however, derived from a Tetrad, but under different names. For they put Pro-arche (Before the Beginning) first, Anennœtos (Inconceivable) second, Arrhetos (Indescribable) third, Aoratos (Invisible) fourth. Then after Pro-arche they say Arche (Beginning) came forth and occupied the first and the fifth place; from Anennœtos came Acataleptos (Incomprehensible) in the second and the sixth place; from Arrhetos came Anonomastos (Nameless) in the third and the seventh place; from Aoratos came Agennetos (Unbegotten) in the fourth and the eight place. Now by what method he arranges this, that each of these Æons should be born in two places, and that, too, at such intervals, I prefer to be ignorant of than to be informed. For what can be right in a system which is propounded with such absurd particulars?

Chapter XXXVI.—Less Reprehensible Theories in the Heresy. Bad is the Best of Valentinianism.

How much more sensible are they who, rejecting all this tiresome nonsense, have refused to believe that any one Æon has descended from another by steps like these, which are really neither more nor less Gemonian; but that on a given signal the eight-fold emanation, of which we have heard, issued all at once from the Father and His Ennœa (Thought),—that it is, in fact, from His mere motion that they gain their designations. When, as they say, He thought of producing offspring, He on that account gained the name of Father. After producing, because the issue which He produced was true, He received the name of Truth. When He wanted Himself to be manifested, He on that account was announced as Man. Those, moreover, whom He preconceived in His thought when He produced them, were then designated the Church. As man, He uttered His Word; and so this Word is His first-begotten Son, and to the Word was added Life. And by this process the first Ogdoad was completed. However, the whole of this tiresome story is utterly poor and weak.

Chapter XXXVII.—Other Turgid and Ridiculous Theories About the Origin of the Æons and Creation, Stated and Condemned.

Now listen to some other buffooneries of a master who is a great swell among them, and who has pronounced his dicta with an even priestly authority. They run thus: There comes, says he, before all things Pro-arche, the inconceivable, and indescribable, and nameless, which I for my own part call Monotes (Solitude). With this was associated another power, to which also I give the name of Henotes (Unity). Now, inasmuch as Monotes and Henotes—that is to say, Solitude and Union—were only one being, they produced, and yet not in the way of production, the intellectual, innascible, invisible beginning of all things, which human language has called Monad (Solitude). This has inherent in itself a consubstantial force, which it calls Unity These powers, accordingly, Solitude or Solitariness, and Unity, or Union, propagated all the other emanations of Æons. Wonderful distinction, to be sure! Whatever change Union and Unity may undergo; Solitariness and Solitude is profoundly supreme. Whatever designation you give the power, it is one and the same.

Chapter XXXVIII.—Diversity in the Opinions of Secundus, as Compared with the General Doctrine of Valentinus.

Secundus is a trifle more human, as he is briefer: he divides the Ogdoad into a pair of Tetrads, a right hand one and a left hand one, one light and the other darkness. Only he is unwilling to derive the power which apostatized and fell away from any one of the Æons, but from the fruits which issued from their substance.

Chapter XXXIX.—Their Diversity of Sentiment Affects the Very Central Doctrine of Christianity, Even the Person and Character of the Lord Jesus. This Diversity Vitiates Every Gnostic School.

Now, concerning even the Lord Jesus, into how great a diversity of opinion are they divided! One party form Him of the blossoms of all the Æons. Another party will have it that He is made up only of those ten whom the Word and the Life produced; from which circumstance the titles of the Word and the Life were suitably transferred to Him. Others, again, that He rather sprang from the twelve, the offspring of Man and the Church, and therefore, they say, He was designated "Son of man." Others, moreover, maintain that He was formed by Christ and the Holy Spirit, who have to provide for the establishment of the universe, and that He inherits by right His Father's appellation. Some there are who have imagined that another origin must be found for the title "Son of man;" for they have had the presumption to call the Father Himself Man, by reason of the profound mystery of this title: so that what can you hope for more ample concerning faith in that God, with whom you are now yourself on a par? Such conceits are constantly cropping out amongst them, from the redundance of their mother's seed. And so it happens that the doctrines which have grown up amongst the Valentinians have already extended their rank growth to the woods of the Gnostics.

www.ingramcontent.com/pod-product-compliance
Lightning Source LLC
Chambersburg PA
CBHW071014120726
47910CB00004B/1515
* 9 7 8 1 6 4 3 7 3 0 8 5 1 *